OSTRICHES

LIVING WILD

Published by Creative Education and Creative Paperbacks
P.O. Box 227, Mankato, Minnesota 56002
Creative Education and Creative Paperbacks are imprints of The Creative Company
www.thecreativecompany.us

Design and production by Mary Herrmann
Art direction by Rita Marshall
Printed in China

Photographs by Creative Commons Wikimedia (Donna Brown, Christophe Eyquem, Luis García, Harrogate Museums and Arts, Lip Kee, Wen-Cheng Liu, MathKnight, G.D. Rowley, Michael Schmid, Syrian painter c. 1335), Getty Images (Florilegius), iStockphoto (aimee1065, brazzo, Casarsa, gorsh13, gynane, JohnCarnemolla, JoseIgnacioSoto, Wojciech Kozielczyk, Enrique Ramos Lopez, pjmalsbury, Nailia Schwarz, skibreck, Valmol48), Shutterstock (06photo, airobody, Stacey Ann Alberts, alfotokunst, Artush, CreativeNature, jo Crebbin, Dominique de La Croix, Flipser, Chris Fourie, Four Oaks, fullempty, Elsa Hoffmann, Roland Ijdema, JelenaDiazPhotography, Andrzej Kubik, Alta Oosthuizen, Stephanie Periquet, R.Zwerver, svic, Mogens Trolle)

Library of Congress Cataloging-in-Publication Data
Gish, Melissa.
Ostriches / Melissa Gish.
p. cm. — (Living wild)
Includes bibliographical references and index.
Summary: A look at ostriches, including their habitats, physical characteristics such as long and powerful legs, behaviors, relationships with humans, and their herd hierarchy in the world today.

ISBN 978-1-60818-706-5 (hardcover)
ISBN 978-1-62832-302-3 (pbk)
ISBN 978-1-56660-742-1 (eBook)
1. Ostriches—Juvenile literature. 2. Ostriches—Folklore—Juvenile literature. I. Title.

QL696.S9 G55 2016
598.5/24—dc23   2015026878

CCSS: RI.5.1, 2, 3, 8; RST.6-8.1, 2, 5, 6, 8; RH.6-8.3, 4, 5, 6, 7, 8

First Edition HC 9 8 7 6 5 4 3 2 1
First Edition PBK 9 8 7 6 5 4 3 2 1

CREATIVE EDUCATION • CREATIVE PAPERBACKS

OSTRICHES

Melissa Gish

The sun is setting on Ethiopia's Yabello National Park.
A female ostrich rises from her nest to let her

male partner take watch over their eggs by night.

he sun is setting on Ethiopia's Yabello National Park. A female ostrich rises from her nest to let her male partner take watch over their eggs by night. She ruffles her feathers, shaking off the day's dust, and heads off to feed. Using his wide beak, the male begins turning all 20 of the eggs, pausing occasionally to scan the area. It is late May, the end of the dry season, and lightning flashes in the distance. The ostrich

spies movement: a troop of hamadryas baboons. He faces the baboons and spreads his feathers in a show of force. Several baboons break away from the troop and circle to the ostrich's back. Their plan is a simple one—to distract the bird and steal the eggs. But the ostrich is alert. He whirls and chases the intruders. The baboons scatter. No eggs tonight. This ostrich is far too vigilant to be tricked.

WHERE IN THE WORLD THEY LIVE

■ **Masai Ostrich**
eastern Africa

■ **Red-necked Ostrich**
northern Africa

■ **Southern Ostrich**
southern Africa

■ **Somali Ostrich**
Horn of Africa region

The largest birds in the world cannot fly, but they roam the grasslands of the African continent. Common ostriches are categorized into three subspecies: North African (or red-necked) ostriches range across the countries of northern Africa, while Masai ostriches are found in the east, and southern ostriches inhabit the south. Somali ostriches are a separate species native to the Horn of Africa, near the Arabian Sea. The colored squares represent some common locations of each of the subspecies and species living in the wild today.

BIGGER, FASTER, BOLDER

Unlike their plains-dwelling ostrich relatives, bold-colored cassowaries live in forested regions.

Ostriches are not only the largest birds in the world, but they are also the fastest feathered runners. They can run 45 miles (72.4 km) per hour steadily for 30 minutes, but ostriches cannot fly. Like other birds, ostriches are warm-blooded, feathered, beaked animals that walk on two feet and lay eggs. The two ostrich species make up the entire order Struthioniformes. This name is Greek for "sparrow wings" and likely refers to the fact that an ostrich's wings are small in relation to its body size. The closest relatives of the ostrich include large birds such as the emu, rhea, and cassowary, as well as the smaller kiwi. These flightless birds are included with the ostrich in a group known as the ratites. The word "ratite" derives from the Greek word for "raft." A raft lacks a keel—the blade-shaped structure that keeps a watercraft upright—and can only float on water. Similarly, ratites do not have the blade-shaped breastbone to which flight muscles are attached. Ratites' breastbones are flat, like rafts, so these birds cannot sail through the air—they can only run on the ground.

The Somali ostrich's neck and legs are gray-blue, rather than pink like other ostriches'.

Ostriches will nab lizards, snakes, or small rodents that come within easy reach for a quick protein boost.

The two ostrich species (including three subspecies of common ostriches) are found only in Africa. The North African ostrich, commonly called the red-necked ostrich, ranges throughout six countries from Mauritania to Sudan. Two other subspecies of common ostrich are the Masai ostrich (found in Ethiopia, parts of southern Somalia, southern Kenya, and eastern Tanzania) and the southern ostrich (found only in southern Africa). The Somali ostrich, declared a separate species in 2014, inhabits Somalia, southern Ethiopia, Djibouti, and northeastern Kenya. An additional subspecies, the Arabian ostrich, was hunted to **extinction** by the mid-20th century.

The red-necked is the largest ostrich. This ostrich can stand 9 feet (2.7 m) tall from head to toe and weigh more than 300 pounds (136 kg). Other ostriches average 7 to 8 feet (2.1–2.4 m) in height and typically weigh 200 to 230 pounds (90.7–104 kg). Because of their size, ostriches have no natural enemies. Even lions keep their distance. These large birds can deliver a forward kick with 2,000 pounds of pressure per square inch (141 kg/cm^2)—more than twice the force of a professional boxer's punch. One kick is strong enough to break a

About 70 red-necked ostriches are part of a species recovery program in northern Niger.

Rheas are ostrich cousins native to the pampas, or open grasslands, of South America.

lion's back. While young ostriches are vulnerable to predators, their parents are fiercely protective, and other animals know it.

Like most birds, ostriches exhibit sexual dimorphism, which means males and females differ in appearance. In the case of ostriches, males are about one-quarter larger than their female counterparts and have more visually striking feathers, called plumage. Males are generally black with white tips on their wings and tails, and females are dull gray or brown in color. Males' plumage makes them attractive to females, while females' plumage provides them with **camouflage** in their dry, grassy, and sandy habitat. Ostriches regulate their body temperature by fluffing their feathers, which either traps or releases pockets of air close to their bodies.

Ostriches have long necks and long legs that help them avoid direct heat steaming up from the hot, dry ground. The neck and head are nearly featherless, covered with only a thin layer of **down**. The legs are bare, with the upper legs covered with pink skin and the lower legs covered with thick scales. The knees are located behind the ribs, and the ankles (partway

Male ostriches sport much darker feathers than their female counterparts.

Unlike most birds, ostriches' feathers are not protected by a waterproof coating, so a heavy rain will soak them.

Ostriches' feet differ from most other birds', which have three forward-facing toes and one backward toe.

Ostriches have excellent vision and can clearly see objects up to 2.5 miles (4 km) away.

up the legs) bend forward. Unlike other ratites, which have three toes, ostriches have just two. The thick, seven-inch-long (17.8 cm) inner toe is topped with a four-inch-long (10.2 cm) claw resembling a hoof. The outer toe is smaller and is useful for balance when the ostrich is running. Although the ostrich's wings are not made for flight, they provide additional balance, helping ostriches make sharp maneuvers while running.

Ostriches live on **savannas**, where they use their powerful, two-inch-wide (5.1 cm) eyes—the largest of any bird's—to scan the landscape for danger. The ostrich's eye is larger than its brain, and with such a small brain, the ostrich isn't much of a problem solver. While these birds are able to quickly dispatch predators with a solid kick, they prefer to avoid conflict. Unless they are defending a nest or offspring, ostriches usually choose to run away from threats. If they can, they will hide by lying flat on the ground so that they appear to be nothing more than a pile of rock or grass.

Ostriches spend most of their waking hours foraging for food in the form of various plants, grasses, and shrubs. During the savanna's rainy season, which occurs from

Running in groups helps ostriches confuse predators by making it more difficult to pinpoint individual bodies.

Ostriches have a frowning gape—the fleshy part of the mouth where the upper and lower mandibles meet.

late spring to early fall, ostriches enjoy green vegetation and fat insect treats. But during the dry season, ostriches may need to travel many miles to find enough food. An adult ostrich eats approximately seven pounds (3.2 kg) of vegetation daily. Ostriches have an efficient digestive system. Food first passes through the proventriculus (*proh-ven-TRIK-yuh-lus*)—the stomach. This structure contains roughly 300 **glands** that secrete digestive juices that break down food. The material then passes to the ventriculus, or gizzard. This muscle-like organ uses ingested stones and grit to grind solids into liquid mush. Finally, the liquid moves through the 46-foot-long (14 m) intestine, where a high percentage of **nutrients** is absorbed.

In the ostrich's hot climate, every drop of water counts. Because its body can retain most of the moisture from the food it consumes, the ostrich can go long periods of time without drinking water. Other birds defecate and urinate up to 30 times a day, but ostriches do so only 4 or 5 times a day, which helps them conserve moisture. Ostriches also breathe slowly through a two-chambered **nasal** passage that captures water vapor that might otherwise escape each time the birds exhale.

Although they do not need to drink much water, ostriches seek out pools when the weather is especially hot.

At any given time, an adult ostrich typically has 2 to 2.5 pounds (0.9–1.1 kg) of stones in its gizzard.

During mating season, ostrich roosters are highly protective of their harem of hens.

DON'T MESS WITH THE NEST

An ostrich has 17 vertebrae in its neck, which makes bending the neck easier.

Ostriches are social birds that live part of the year with a nesting partner and part of the year in family groups, called herds. Herds include up to 50 individuals, depending on the availability of resources. Males are called roosters, and females are called hens. A dominant rooster leads a herd as the birds forage for food and sleep, with some birds standing guard throughout the night. During mating and nesting season, which lasts about three months during the winter, some of the roosters break away from their herd. They gather three to five mature hens into a harem, or group of mates. Sometimes roosters fight over hens.

A dominant rooster mates only with the hens in his harem. To signal to his hens, the rooster's neck turns bright red, and he makes loud, booming sounds. To impress the hens, a rooster sits down, spreads his wings, and sways from side to side, tossing his head back and forth. Such a powerful display lets the hens know they can count on the rooster to be a good father. When a hen accepts the rooster's proposal, she crouches down, drooping her spread wings, and pecks at the ground as

If a female is pleased with a male's courtship dance, she will make a clapping sound with her beak.

she moves toward him. These dances and displays may continue for days before mating occurs.

One of the hens, typically the oldest, is the dominant hen. She is always the first to mate and lay eggs, and she and the rooster will ultimately be responsible for rearing the entire harem's offspring. Together, they dig a shallow impression in the dirt. The dominant hen lays one egg every two days until she has about a dozen. Strict **hierarchy** keeps nesting organized. Only when the dominant hen allows the lower-ranking females near the nest will they be able to lay eggs. Taking turns, the lower-ranking hens lay up to a dozen eggs each, though younger hens typically lay fewer eggs than older hens. When the nest is full—containing up to 60 eggs—the incubation period can begin.

Ostrich eggs are the largest of any bird's but the smallest in relation to body size. At six inches (15.2 cm) in diameter and about three pounds (1.4 kg), an egg is only about 1.5 percent of an ostrich's body weight. By comparison, the ostrich's cousin, the kiwi of New Zealand, lays an egg that is roughly 25 percent of its body weight. The content of an ostrich egg is equal to about 24 medium chicken eggs. The ostrich's eggshell is very thick—and difficult to open. Baboons often abandon stolen eggs unopened, but predators with crushing jaws leave few remnants behind.

For an average of 42 days, roosters and dominant hens take turns caring for eggs. In the morning and evening, the hen sits on the eggs to keep them warm. Her plumage makes her look like a pile of dirt in the brown grass. In the heat of day, she must stand over the nest to provide shade. She turns the eggs frequently to keep the babies

Ostriches must be ever watchful for predators, since their nests are vulnerable to attack.

If ostriches lie in one position too long, their body weight can pinch nerves in their legs, making their legs go numb.

The hyena's bite—seven times stronger than a human's—is powerful enough to crush ostrich eggs.

By the time they are 1 month old, ostrich chicks can reach running speeds of up to 35 miles (56.3 km) per hour.

inside moist. Lower-ranking hens are sometimes allowed to care for eggs as well. As hens care for the eggs, the male patrols the area and forages for food. Sometimes the dominant female steps away for a few minutes to eat, but she and her mate both keep an eye on the nest and rush back in case of trouble.

At night, the rooster sits on the eggs while the hens go off to feed. The rooster's black plumage makes him invisible in the dark. He turns the eggs periodically. At dawn, the dominant hen returns to trade places. For six weeks, the ostrich pair continues this ritual—getting very little sleep. Despite the parents' vigilance, predators such as baboons, hyenas, vultures, and wild dogs raid about 90 percent of ostrich nests. If a nest is destroyed, ostriches can sometimes lay more eggs, but often they must wait until the next year to try again.

When the time comes to hatch, the babies inside begin vocalizing. They chirp continuously so that their parents will learn their voices. Using its **egg tooth**, a hatchling chips through the hard shell of its egg. It pushes with its legs, resting periodically, until the shell is broken apart. Sometimes the effort is too much. Because only the

Upon hatching, baby ostriches are roughly the size of full-grown chickens.

Both parents must remain close to their chicks in order to offer their family the best protection.

strongest birds hatch, about 30 percent of baby ostriches never make it out of the egg. Hatchlings are 12 inches (30.5 cm) tall and weigh 2 pounds (0.9 kg). They can walk within a few hours. At first, the hatchlings are covered with brown speckled down, but these fluffy feathers soon grow darker and thicker. Within two weeks, spiky feathers, called pinfeathers, emerge.

For the first few days of life, ostrich chicks are sustained by a substance in their egg yolk called vitelline (*VIT-uh-lin*). Watching their parents, the chicks then practice pecking for food. Early on, they may peck rocks, sticks, and even lizards, learning these things are not tasty to eat. When they pluck leaves from shrubs and seeds from grass, they discover the best food sources. Both parents stay close to the nest and chicks. Baboons, hyenas, lions, jackals, leopards, and snakes hunt young ostriches. If a predator comes too close, the hen will sit down with all the chicks gathered underneath her while the rooster chases the intruder away or attacks it with his killer kick.

When ostrich chicks get bigger, ostrich families come back together in herds. The birds find additional safety in numbers when chicks grow too big to seek protection under their parents' wings. As they grow during their first year—up to three inches (7.6 cm) per week—the chicks continue to require their parents' protection. Still, only 15 percent of chicks survive their first year. Predators, as well as food shortages and infections, claim the lives of many young ostriches. Those that survive match their parents in size within a year, but they require an additional six months to develop their full adult plumage. Juvenile ostriches stay with their family group for another two to three years—until they are ready to have offspring of their own. An ostrich's life span is roughly 30 years.

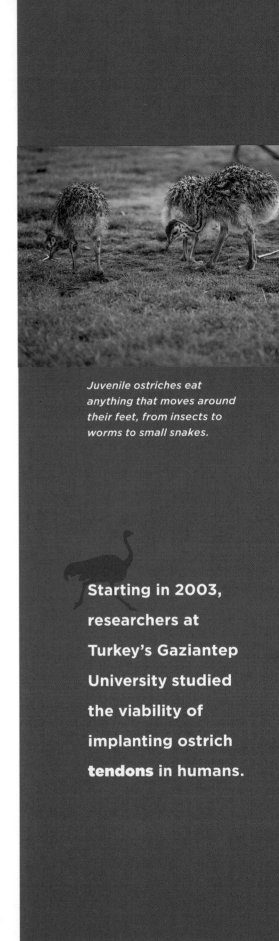

Juvenile ostriches eat anything that moves around their feet, from insects to worms to small snakes.

Starting in 2003, researchers at Turkey's Gaziantep University studied the viability of implanting ostrich tendons in humans.

The idea that ostriches bury their heads in the ground is the result of simple misperception.

GET YOUR HEAD OUT OF THE SAND

Around 3500 B.C., people on the banks of Egypt's Nile River painted ostrich images on their pottery.

Perhaps the most common **myth** associated with ostriches is that they bury their heads in the sand when frightened. The myth undoubtedly originated when observers spotted ostriches lying flat on the ground, their necks outstretched and their heads perfectly still on the ground. Ostriches do this to disguise themselves as a pile of rocks or a shrub when protecting a nest—and usually they are quite successful. They do not actually bury their heads, though. Today, when people are accused of "playing ostrich" or "burying their head in the sand," it means they are refusing to face the reality of a situation.

Ostriches have shared the world with people for tens of thousands of years. **Archaeologists** studying the Diepkloof Rock Shelter in Western Cape, South Africa, made an important discovery in 2010. They found nearly 300 ostrich eggshell fragments with decorative patterns etched into the shells. Researchers, led by Dr. Pierre-Jean Texier of France's University of Bordeaux, believe the fragments are 60,000 years old. Scientists previously thought that cave paintings in Europe dating to 40,000 years ago represented the oldest form of human social communication. However,

Traders likely carried this painted ostrich egg from Africa to Spain more than 2,000 years ago.

Ostrich eggs were laid on the graves of soldiers in Ethiopia to show how many enemies the deceased had killed.

scientists now believe the repeating patterns etched into the ostrich eggshells indicate that key traits of human culture emerged much earlier.

According to the mythology of various African cultures—chiefly the Shona people of Zimbabwe and Mozambique, the Shanga of Nigeria, the Swazi of Swaziland and South Africa, and the Zulu of southern Africa—an earth mother goddess spread her blood around the world to make the plants and animals grow. Red ochre (*OH-ker*), a substance made from crushed stones and minerals, came to symbolize the goddess's fertility. The ostrich was a vital component in the use of red ochre. Plain red ochre is chalky and dry, but when mixed with fat cooked off ostrich meat, it becomes an oily paint that stains the skin and provides moisture protection. Early peoples used red ochre to paint on rock walls, decorate costumes, and even cover their hair and bodies to symbolize their connection with the earth mother, who gave them food and kept them healthy.

The Xhosa people of southeastern Africa believed that ostrich oil helped prevent aging and decay. Tribal chiefs were treated to regular massages with ostrich oil to help

them stay young, and dead bodies were covered with oil to help them be reborn in the afterlife. Even today, many people believe that ostrich oil can heal dry or burned skin, relieve muscle soreness, and even erase wrinkles. Some uses of ostrich oil have been scientifically confirmed, while others remain unproven. A team of medical researchers led by Dr. Gan Seng Chiew of the Universiti Tunku Abdul Rahman in Malaysia is studying the use of ostrich oil to

The 8th-century Arab al-Jāhiz wrote about creatures he encountered, such as the now-extinct Arabian ostrich.

THE STORY OF AN OSTRICH

A robust old ostrich, with head little bigger
Than that of some creatures of far frailer figure,
With two legs complete, and a speed very fleet,
Once caught a short peep at his feet, in the street.

So far from his head did they seem to be located,
He failed to take note that upon each were notated
Scales, warts and abrasions, nails, ossification,
Which proved them a part of his own corporation.

He noticed, however, wherever he went,
They came along, too, and he asked what it meant?
Though he walked through the town, or he stalked
  o'er the heath
He observed they remained, always, right underneath.
He thrust out his bust and inside he just cussed,
When they strode along and kept kicking up dust;
But in vain did he feign to abstain from disdain,
As he dined with the twain in the wind and the rain;
Or stared around therein, while wearing a bear-grin,
Evincing an evident, ill-concealed chagrin....

from The Story of an Ostrich: An Allegory and
Humorous Satire in Rhyme, *by Judd Isaacs, c. 1903*

treat arthritis, a disease affecting the joints. The team's tests conducted in 2010 showed promising results.

Since ancient times, ostrich feathers have been desired for their unique look and feel. The ancient Egyptians saw them as symbols of justice and buried them in the tombs of their kings and queens. In Africa and the Middle East, tribal leaders wore robes and headdresses adorned with ostrich feathers. In Europe, feathers were used as symbols of power that topped the helmets of military leaders. By the 19th century, ostrich feathers had become popular in ladies' fashions, particularly in hats and in scarves known as boas. In the late 1800s, ostrich feathers shipped from Africa were nearly as valuable as the diamonds mined on that continent. Today, ostrich feathers are used for a variety of purposes, from dusters and decorative lampshades to fancy fans and masks. Though less popular than in centuries past, ostrich feathers are still used in women's clothing—particularly wedding dresses that feature hundreds of white feathers.

An ostrich egg is at the center of a 500-year-old mystery. In 2012, an Austrian map collector acquired a globe made from two bottom halves of ostrich eggs glued together to form a sphere. The egg is etched in

Tutankhamen's tomb was uncovered in 1922 by British archaeologist Howard Carter.

A carved wooden fan showing King Tut hunting ostriches was found in the Egyptian ruler's tomb in 1922.

Exotic species such as ostriches are celebrated and preserved in Ukraine's Askania-Nova reserve.

Ostriches' long "eyelashes" are in fact fine feathers useful for keeping dust out of the birds' eyes.

great detail. The New World (the Americas) appears as a collection of islands, and the Latin phrase *Hic Sunt Dracones*—Here Be Dragons—appears in the area of Southeast Asia. What makes this egg-globe so special is its age. Scholars believe it was crafted in 1504, making it the oldest known globe to include the New World. However, they are still trying to figure out who made it.

In modern times, fictional ostriches are typically depicted as tall, awkward characters. One of the most recognizable ostrich characters is the ballerina Madame Upanova, who, with her troupe of ostrich ballerinas, was featured in the 1940 Walt Disney classic *Fantasia*. Although the ostriches were all female, they were given black and white male plumage. Madame Upanova also made a brief appearance in the movie *Who Framed Roger Rabbit?* (1988), and she appeared in *Disney's House of Mouse*, a television show that ran from 2001 to 2003. The first Walt Disney ostrich was Hortense, the beloved pet of Donald Duck, who was introduced in the 1937 short film *Donald's Ostrich*. Over the years, Hortense appeared in 23 Donald Duck comics.

Walter Lantz Productions, creator of such beloved bird characters as Chilly Willy and Woody Woodpecker,

produced the 1957 cartoon *The Ostrich Egg and I*, in which a man named Sam hatches an ostrich that proceeds to eat everything in sight. He tries to get rid of the pesky bird but ends up with a houseful of baby ostriches instead. Sam's ostrich behaves a bit like real ostriches in captivity. Ostriches exhibit curiosity about things that move or shimmer, but with small brains, they are not very discerning. They often try to taste shiny objects. Captive ostriches have been known to eat nails, barbed wire, and hinges. Such objects typically kill ostriches, but sometimes they survive their dangerous diet!

English naturalist Charles Sketchley opened the first ostrich ranch in the U.S. near Anaheim, California, in 1883.

Wildebeest have no interest in harming ostriches but may be curious about birds sharing water sources.

BIG, BIG BIRDS

Fossils of flightless birds are extremely rare, so scientists theorize as to how prehistoric birds became ostriches. *Palaeotis weigelti* is considered the earliest member of the order Struthioniformes and is believed to be the first direct ostrich ancestor. It lived from about 47 to 41 million years ago. Its fossils were first discovered in Germany in the 1930s. Because few other ratite fossils exist, scientists have turned to **DNA** for answers to the mystery of ratite **evolution**. By comparing the **genes** of many different bird species, scientists have been able to determine which birds are related to one another. A 2010 study led by evolutionary biologist Dr. Matthew Phillips at Australian National University revealed that the first ratites were related to ground-dwelling birds that evolved about 65 million years ago. This was after dinosaurs went extinct but before meat-eating **mammals** emerged.

The time for change was ideal for the chicken-sized birds that had previously flown away from predators. With nothing to eat them, the birds could grow larger and heavier. Big birds need big wings, and it takes a lot

Ostriches are the only birds susceptible to anthrax, a potentially deadly disease usually restricted to sheep and cattle.

The kiwi, the national symbol of New Zealand, lends its name to the term for native New Zealanders.

of energy to fly. But with no need to fly, the evolving ratites could do without flight wings and instead put their energy into growth. Some ratites, such as the kiwi, remained small, but others grew large. When the first big cats arrived in Africa and Asia roughly 25 million years ago, ratites there began to develop stronger legs for running and wider wings for balance. By about 12 million years ago, most ratites had the ability to outrun—and kick to death—their new predators.

The largest ostrich relative—and the largest bird to ever live—was the moa. At least nine species of moa existed in New Zealand from about 40,000 years ago until the 1400s. Standing 12 feet tall (3.7 m) and weighing more than 500 pounds (227 kg), these mild-mannered birds were herbivores, meaning they ate only plant matter. The humans who first settled in New Zealand (the Maori) eventually hunted moas to extinction.

Today, some ostriches are in similar trouble. Scientists fear the Somali ostrich could suffer the same fate as its moa cousins if conservation measures are not increased. A rapid population decline over the last 50 years has led the International Union for Conservation of Nature (IUCN)

to classify the Somali ostrich as vulnerable to extinction. In 2009, **ornithologists** Dr. John D. Atkins and Dr. John Ash documented some of the reasons for the Somali ostrich's decline in numbers. They found that people raid nests and use the eggs as ornaments, water containers, and lucky charms in churches and graves. It was also discovered that people abuse the birds for recreation, shooting them for target practice or chasing them in vehicles until the birds die of exhaustion. And like other ostrich species, the Somali ostrich is heavily hunted for its meat, feathers, and skin. The skin is made into leather.

Scientists estimate that up to 12 million moas were living in New Zealand when the first humans arrived there.

Ostrich herds are nomadic, meaning they travel from place to place in search of resources.

The IUCN classifies red-necked ostriches as a species of least concern because they have a large range and their numbers—at least in captivity—are abundant. Even so, their range has shrunk by more than two-thirds in the last century. Conservationists fear that red-necked ostriches could be eliminated from much, if not all, of their native habitat if issues related to hunting and habitat destruction are not addressed. In northwestern Africa's Republic of Niger, the Aïr (*ah-EER*) Mountains are part of Africa's largest protected area, covering 40,000 square miles (103,600 sq km). Aïr was once home to thousands of red-necked ostriches, but the birds were **poached** out of existence throughout Niger during the 1990s.

In 2004, the Sahara Conservation Fund (SCF) relocated some red-necked ostriches back to Niger, but none of the birds roamed free. Private owners were selected to **captive-breed** them. In 2009 and 2010, in an effort to increase genetic diversity, SCF researchers moved some of the birds from owner to owner to promote interbreeding. The goal has been to rebuild a large enough population to reintroduce a herd of red-necked ostriches to the wild. But the birds will not be released until the SCF is confident that the Nigerien government will provide education and support to protect them. Such efforts could take a long time. A similar program began in Tunisia's Dghoumes National Park in 2008. Today, red-necked ostriches roam free there.

Because ostriches provide valuable meat and leather, they are raised on ostrich ranches around the world. **Domesticated** ostriches have been selectively bred to be smaller than wild ostriches, to have more white feathers,

Rooster Cogburn Ostrich Ranch is a popular roadside attraction near Picacho Peak State Park, in Arizona.

The South African city of Oudtshoorn is the "ostrich capital of the world," with 200,000 birds on 500 ranches.

Despite its softness, ostrich leather is considered one of the most durable types of leather in the world.

and to behave less aggressively. Some ranchers allow ostriches to sit on their eggs and rear their own chicks. Other ranchers collect the eggs daily and incubate them artificially. When her eggs are taken, an ostrich hen keeps laying, often more than 100 eggs in a nesting season. Some ranches are home to hundreds of birds—many more than would normally be found in a herd. Because of their close quarters, domestic ostriches are prone to infections and other diseases. Ranchers must constantly monitor the health of their birds.

Ranchers must also monitor how much their birds eat. In the wild, ostriches walk long distances to find enough food to sustain them daily. On ranches, where space is limited but food is not, ostriches will easily overeat, stuffing their bodies to unhealthy levels. When raising chicks, extra care must be taken. Too many chicks in a confined area can become stressed, which may lead to pecking and cannibalism (the act of eating the same species). Despite the challenges of ostrich ranching, these birds are considered worthy products to buy and sell. Their leather is soft and luxurious, and their meat is high in protein. France is by far the greatest consumer of ostrich meat, purchasing more

than 8 million pounds (3.6 million kg) annually. The North American market is slowly growing.

Not only are ostriches important in Africa's **food chain**, but these birds also provide monetary value to people who raise them. More important, though, is their uniqueness among wildlife. While ostriches may thrive in captivity, many have disappeared from their native wilderness. Education and conservation must be encouraged in order to help ostriches survive and flourish in their natural habitats.

Much of the ostrich's habitat in southwestern Africa is covered with laterite, soil enriched with iron that makes it red.

ANIMAL TALE: OSTRICH'S SECRET FIRE

Various African peoples include regional wildlife in their traditions and stories. The mantis is an important spirit animal in the creation stories of southern Africa's San (a people sometimes known as Bushmen). The praying posture of the mantis—leaning forward with arms bent and head tilted to one side—represents the spirit of the mantis listening to the prayers and requests of the San. This traditional San story tells how the wise ostrich gave up its greatest secret to the mantis—and to humans.

Ostrich was a curious fellow. He was always traveling and exploring. He came to know many things about the land and the sky. But whenever he learned something new, he kept the knowledge secret, for he wanted to be known as the wisest of all the animals.

One day, Ostrich traveled to the highest peak on the most distant mountain. There he learned the origin of fire. He tested the fire, setting the tall grass ablaze and then stomping out the flames with his powerful feet. *What a wonderful treasure*, thought Ostrich. He tucked the fire under his wing and carried it home.

One day, Mantis was passing by and saw Ostrich cooking meat on an open fire. Mantis had never seen fire before, so he stopped to ask Ostrich what it was. "That looks like it would be most useful to the humans," Mantis said to Ostrich.

"They cannot have it," replied Ostrich. "It is my secret." And with that, he quickly picked up the fire and tucked it under his wing to hide it. "Now go on your way," he said to Mantis.

All night, Mantis pondered the many uses of the fire he had seen. He knew it would be useful to humans and wanted to share it with them. But how would he get it from Ostrich, who kept it tucked tightly under his wing? He thought and thought. And then he came up with a plan.

The next morning, Mantis went to see Ostrich. "I know where we can find the finest figs in the land," Mantis told Ostrich, for he knew that figs were Ostrich's favorite fruit.

"Where?" Ostrich asked eagerly.

"You must follow me," Mantis said, "and I will show you."

Ostrich bobbed his head, smiling, and followed Mantis. Soon, they came to a grove of fig trees. "There," said Mantis, pointing to the tallest of the trees. "The finest figs grow on that tree." Ostrich stretched his neck and began plucking the delicious, juicy figs from the tree. "Up there," Mantis said. "The better figs are higher up." So Ostrich reached even farther.

"Go higher," Mantis said to Ostrich. "The very best figs are very high." Ostrich could not stretch his neck any more, so he raised his wings over his head to grasp the finest figs from the uppermost branches. As he stuffed his mouth with fruit, the fire slipped from its hiding place under his wing and fell to the ground.

Mantis immediately snatched it up and flew away to share it with the humans. At first, Ostrich was angry, but then he realized that it was his own greed that had allowed him to be tricked. He felt so foolish that, to this day, Ostrich holds his wings close to his body so that no one can steal secrets from him again.

GLOSSARY

archaeologists – people who study human history by examining ancient peoples and their artifacts

camouflage – the ability to hide, due to coloring or markings that blend in with a given environment

captive-breed – breed and raise in a place from which escape is not possible

DNA – deoxyribonucleic acid; a substance found in every living thing that determines the species and individual characteristics of that thing

domesticated – tamed to be kept as a pet or used as a work animal

down – small feathers whose barbs do not interlock to form a flat surface, thus giving a fluffy appearance

egg tooth – a hard, toothlike tip of a young bird's beak or a young reptile's mouth, used only for breaking through its egg

evolution – the process of adapting to survive in a certain environment

extinction – the act or process of becoming extinct; coming to an end or dying out

food chain – a system in nature in which living things are dependent on each other for food

genes – the basic physical units of heredity

glands – organs in a human or animal body that produce chemical substances used by other parts of the body

hierarchy – a system in which people, animals, or things are ranked in importance one above another

mammals – warm-blooded animals that have a backbone and hair or fur, give birth to live young, and produce milk to feed their young

myth – a popular, traditional belief or story that explains how something came to be or that is associated with a person or object

nasal – relating to the nose

nutrients – substances that give an animal energy and help it grow

ornithologists – scientists who study birds and their lives

poached – hunted protected species of wild animals, even though doing so was against the law

savannas – grassy, mostly treeless plains in tropical or subtropical regions

tendons – tough, inelastic tissues that connect muscle to bone

SELECTED BIBLIOGRAPHY

Davies, Stephen. *Ratites and Tinamous*. Oxford: Oxford University Press, 2002.

Donegan, Keenan. "*Struthio camelus*." Animal Diversity Web. http://animaldiversity.org/accounts/Struthio_camelus.

Leifert, Harvey. "Back from the Brink." *Smithsonian Zoogoer,* November/December 2009. http://nationalzoo.si.edu /Publications/Zoogoer/2009/6/BackFromTheBrink.cfm.

McGavin, George. *Endangered: Wildlife on the Brink of Extinction*. Buffalo, N.Y.: Firefly Books, 2006.

National Geographic. "Ostrich." http://animals .nationalgeographic.com/animals/birds/ostrich.

Williams, Edgar. *Ostrich*. London: Reaktion Books, 2013.

Note: Every effort has been made to ensure that any websites listed above were active at the time of publication. However, because of the nature of the Internet, it is impossible to guarantee that these sites will remain active indefinitely or that their contents will not be altered.

Ostriches must compete with humans for space and resources in their native lands.

INDEX